A Mother's Love

D0107573

CONTENTS

❁

II

Endearments from Daughters

III
Endearments from Sons

A Mother's Love

CLASSIC POEMS
celebrating the
MATERNAL HEART

COLLECTED BY

KATHLEEN BLEASE

FAWCETT BOOKS

The Ballantine Publishing Group • *New York*

A Fawcett Book
Published by The Ballantine Publishing Group

Introduction and compilation copyright © 1999 by The Ballantine Publishing Group, a division of Random House, Inc.

All rights reserved under International and Pan-American Copyright Conventions. Published in the United States by The Ballantine Publishing Group, a division of Random House, Inc., New York, and simultaneously in Canada by Random House of Canada Limited, Toronto.

Fawcett and colophon are registered trademarks of Random House, Inc.

www.randomhouse.com/BB/

Library of Congress Cataloging-in-Publication Data
A mother's love : classic poems celebrating the maternal heart / collected by Kathleen Blease. — 1st ed.
p. cm.
Includes indexes.
ISBN 0-449-00545-3
1. Mother and child—Poetry. 2. Motherhood—Poetry.
3. Mothers—Poetry. 4. American poetry. 5. English poetry.
I. Blease, Kathleen.
PS595.M64M696   1999
811.008'03520431—dc21   98-51979

Cover design by Heather Kern

Manufactured in the United States of America

First Edition: May 1999

10   9   8   7   6   5   4   3   2   1

FOR MY MOTHER,

Flora

Acknowledgments

❀

WRITERS OVER THE generations, the masters and those less celebrated alike, are truly responsible for this collection. Nevertheless, this project required the cooperation, energy, and inspiration of others. My gratitude goes to my friend, colleague, and editor Elizabeth Zack for proposing the idea, then giving me the freedom to develop it.

I would like to extend a special thank-you to my husband, my mother, and my two boys. My husband, Roger, offers his support and encouragement and cares for the children and the house at a moment's notice. He is truly my blessing. My mother, Flora, has always encouraged me to continue writing and researching (and learning!) while raising my family. I know firsthand, too, that my mother is the true supermom, dedicating herself to raising her family and making a home while developing her own interests and skills. Thank you for your example of motherhood! As for my boys, Ben and Max, they are the single reason I can experience all the wonders and splendid challenges motherhood brings. Without all they give me, I would not have had the insight to bring this collection to fruition.

Finally, I can't let this moment pass without showing my appreciation to the writers whose verses have endured the test of time and fill these pages. Once again, they are watching us enjoy their wisdom, and I'd like to thank them personally for their immortal inspiration.

INTRODUCTION

❀

ONE MIRACULOUS DAY, you became a mother. Just moments before, nestled warm in your womb, the little wonder—the child you had never seen but already knew well—filled your heart with anticipation. Then, on that day, that difficult but glorious day, your delicate creation finally laid snug in your arms, against your skin. Warm. Soft. Innocent. Love for this new person filled you instantly and made you complete, never wanting to return to living without it. And so began your new, lifelong journey as a mother.

How sweetly your child longs for you as he grows and explores this world. Even as the years go by and he builds a life of independence and embarks on raising his own children, his mother's comfort is deeply desired and well sought. And it is little wonder: He began as a tiny individual tucked under your heart where he grew, cell by cell, until he was ready for the world. All the while your heartbeat lulled him to sleep, and the sway of your body gave him rhythmic comfort, cradled in warmth. Your voice was the first to touch the baby's ears. Perhaps, then, it is biologically built into us to seek our mothers for comfort—for life! Emily E. Judson (see page 71) wrote:

———

Give me my old seat, mother,
With my head upon thy knee;
I've pass'd through many a changing scene
Since thus I sat by thee.
Oh! let me look into thine eyes—
Their meek, soft, loving light
Falls, like a gleam of holiness,
Upon my heart to-night.

Without a doubt, motherhood is a profession that comes with high stakes and no monetary or materialistic gains. Yet it is often the most desired occupation in the world and it can be the most powerful position one could ever hold. As a mother, you hold the key to shaping a child's concepts of what is right and wrong, good and evil, constructive and destructive. And it's this child, molded by your love and your lessons, who grows into a productive adult and builds her corner of the world, affecting everything that touches it. As William Ross Wallace put it so beautifully (see page 101):

(see page 101)

Infancy's the tender fountain,
Power may with beauty flow,
Mother's first to guide the streamlets,
From them souls unresting grow—
Grow on for the good or evil,
Sunshine streamed or evil hurled;
For the hand that rocks the cradle
Is the hand that rules the world.

Many of the great men and women who have changed our world testify to the power of their mothers.

———

"My mother was the most beautiful woman I ever saw," George Washington attested. "All I am I owe to my mother. I attribute all my success in life to the moral, intellectual, and physical education I received from her." So many good things are here on earth because of the loving care of mothers!

Motherhood is an endless task that requires self-lessness, something that can come from only love and commitment. It is a daily act that is admittedly frustrating and exhausting, at times feeling like a heavy chore. But a mother will endure and find new, inventive ways to lighten the load. Besides, the returns are priceless, albeit intangible. How do we determine the value of the first time a child squeals, "Mama!," his little arms wrapped around his mother's neck, a wet kiss planted on her cheek? A mother would walk across deserts and give away every dollar and cent to feel her child safe in her arms.

There's no better time to raise children. With today's technology we can spend more time providing one-on-one affection and attention than any other mothers in history. Still, it is a mother's warm, loving words and her deepest understanding of her offspring that molds a child's universe. Even in this age of technology and information, a mother's love is in high demand—and it will be forever.

Being a mother requires so much physical and spiritual energy that we often have little left to sort out and appreciate the emotions of raising a child, and of being a child. It is a great gift, then, to read words that express the emotions completely, offering you enlightenment and even some empathy from across the generations. Here in this one tiny volume, poets capture all a mother experiences and everything about her her children treasure. *A Mother's Love* features poems from mothers, daughters, and sons. Many poets explore both motherhood and childhood and so eloquently capture the powerful bond between mother and child. To all mothers, and to all who love them: enjoy!

I

Sweet
Thoughts and
Remembrances

LITTLE SARAH

Ye who though unseen are near,
Guard her from all harm,
Watch her well, encompass her
With every potent charm;
Bend above her slumbers,
Kiss her waking eye,
Soothe with your sweet numbers
Each feeble infant cry.

Away from every danger
Besetting baby feet
Turn her little footsteps far,
Guardian angels sweet:
Ever on her quiet lot
Your watchful gazes keep;
Shadow her and shelter her,
Waking or asleep.

BESSIE RAYNER BELLOC
[1829–1925]

MOTHER'S TREASURES

Two little children sit by my side,
I call them Lily and Daffodil;
I gaze on them with a mother's pride,
One is Edna, the other is Will.

Both have eyes of starry light,
And laughing lips o'er teeth of pearl.
I would not change for a diadem
My noble boy and darling girl.

To-night my heart o'erflows with joy;
I hold them as a sacred trust;
I fain would hide them in my heart,
Safe from tarnish of moth and rust.

What should I ask for my dear boy?
The richest gifts of wealth or fame?
What for my girl? A loving heart
And a fair and a spotless name?

What for my boy? That he should stand
A pillar of strength to the state?
What for my girl? That she should be
The friend of the poor and desolate?

I do not ask they shall never tread
With weary feet the paths of pain.
I ask that in the darkest hour
They may faithful and true remain.

I only ask their lives may be
Pure as gems in the gates of pearl,
Lives to brighten and bless the world—
This I ask for my boy and girl.

I ask to clasp their hands again
'Mid the holy hosts of heaven,
Enraptured say:"I am here, oh! God,
"And the children Thou hast given."

FRANCES E. W. HARPER
[1825–1911]

5

TO A LITTLE INVISIBLE BEING WHO IS EXPECTED SOON TO BECOME VISIBLE

❁

Germ of new life, whose powers expanding slow
For many a moon their full perfection wait,—
Haste, precious pledge of happy love, to go
Auspicious borne through life's mysterious gate.

What powers lie folded in thy curious frame,—
Senses from objects locked, and mind from thought!
How little canst thou guess thy lofty claim
To grasp at all the worlds the Almighty wrought!

And see, the genial season's warmth to share,
Fresh younglings shoot, and opening roses glow!
Swarms of new life exulting fill the air,—
Haste, infant bud of being, haste to blow!

For thee the nurse prepares her lulling songs,
The eager matrons count the lingering day;
But far the most thy anxious parent longs
On thy soft cheek a mother's kiss to lay.

She only asks to lay her burden down,
That her glad arms that burden may resume;
And nature's sharpest pangs her wishes crown,
That free thee living from thy living tomb.

———

She longs to fold to her maternal breast
Part of herself, yet to herself unknown;
To see and to salute the stranger guest,
Fed with her life through many a tedious moon.

Come, reap thy rich inheritance of love!
Bask in the fondness of a Mother's eye!
Nor wit nor eloquence her heart shall move
Like the first accents of thy feeble cry.

Haste, little captive, burst thy prison doors!
Launch on the living world, and spring to light!
Nature for thee displays her various stores,
Opens her thousand inlets of delight.

If charmed verse or muttered prayers had power,
With favouring spells to speed thee on thy way,
Anxious I'd bid my beads each passing hour,
Till thy wished smile thy mother's pangs o'erpay.

ANNA LAETITIA BARBAULD
[1743–1825]

———

7

THE BABY'S THOUGHTS

"I wonder what the baby thinks.
Just see how wide awake she lies,
And crows at me, and chirps, and winks,
With laughing wonder in her eyes."

I'll answer for her, little girl.—
"Whose can it be, that merry face,
With hair like sunbeams in a curl,
That hangs around my nestling-place?

"At three months old I've much to learn,
For everything looks strange to me.
But then I know enough to turn
To all the brightest things I see.

"Red roses on the curtain grow,
Once, when't was up, I saw a star.
I wonder, Brown Eyes, if you know
How many splendid things there are?

"Now don't you wish you weren't so tall?
Then you'd live in a cradle, too,
And talk to shadows on the wall,
And think you heard them talk to you.

"But, then, I couldn't spare you, dear;
For when I wake from pretty dreams,
And that great sun goes by, so near,
You seem like one of his soft beams.

"I guess that you, and mother too,
Are pieces broken from the sun.
No; she's the sun, a sunbeam you;
For when she goes, away you run.

"I lie here guessing every day
What all the things around can be;
This four-walled world in which I stay
Is full of wonders, dear, to me."—

There, little girl, your sunny face
Will give the baby thoughts like these;
Then let no frown your brow disgrace,
But be the loveliest thing she sees.

LUCY LARCOM
[1824–1893]

THE MOTHER'S PRAYER

*D*ear Lord, dear Lord,
Thou, who didst not erst deny
The mother-joy to Mary mild
Blessed in the blessed Child—
Hearkening in meek babyhood
Her cradle hymn, albeit used
To all that music interfused
In breasts of angels high and good.
Oh, take not, Lord, my babe away—
Oh, take not to thy songful heaven,
The pretty babe thou hast given;
Or ere that I have seen him play
Around his father's knees, and known
That he knew how my love hath gone
From all the world to him.

ELIZABETH BARRETT BROWNING
[1806–1861]

THE MOTHER

*L*ast night he lay within my arm,
So small, so warm, a mystery
To which God only held the key—
But mine to keep from fear and harm!
Ah! He was all my own, last night,
With soft, persuasive, baby eyes,
So wondering and yet so wise,
And hands that held my finger tight.
Why was it that he could not stay—
Too rare a gift? Yet who could hold
A treasure with securer fold
Than I, to whom love taught the way?
As with a flood of golden light
The first sun tipped earth's golden rim,
So all my world grew bright with him
And with his going fell the night—
O God, is there an angel arm
More strong, more tender than the rest?
Lay Thou my baby on his breast,
To keep him safe from fear and harm!

ISABEL ECCLESTONE MACKAY
[1875–1928]

FROM THE LITTLE HAND

Thou wak'st, my baby boy, from sleep,
And through its silken fringe
Thine eye, like violet, pure and deep,
Gleams forth with azure tinge.

With what a smile of gladness meek
Thy radiant brow is drest,
While fondly to a mother's cheek
Thy lip and hand are prest!

That little hand! what prescient wit
Its history may discern,
When time its tiny bones hath knit
With manhood's sinews stern?

The artist's pencil shall it guide?
Or spread the adventurous sail?
Or guide the plough with rustic pride,
And ply the sounding flail?
. . . .
Yet, oh! may that Almighty Friend,
From whom existence came,
That dear and powerless hand defend
From deeds of guilt and shame.

Grant it to dry the tear of woe,
Bold folly's course restrain,
The alms of sympathy bestow,
The righteous cause maintain—

Write wisdom on the wing of time,
Even 'mid the morn of youth,
And with benevolence sublime
Dispense the light of truth—

Discharge a just, a useful part
Through life's uncertain maze,
Till coupled with an angel's heart,
It strike the lyre of praise.

L. H. SIGOURNEY
[1791–1865]

————

FROM MOTHER AND DAUGHTER:
AN UNCOMPLETED SONNET-SEQUENCE
(SONNETS V, XX, XXV, XXVI, AND XXVII)

V

*L*ast night the broad blue lightnings flamed the sky;
  We watched, our breaths caught as each burst its way,
  And through its fire out-leaped the sharp white ray,
And sudden dark re-closed when it went by:
But she, that where we are will needs be nigh,
  Had tired with hunting orchids half the day.
  Her father thought she called us; he and I,
Half anxious, reached the bedroom where she lay.

Oh lily face upon the whiteness blent!
  How calm she lay in her unconscious grace!
A peal crashed on the silence ere we went;
  She stirred in sleep, a little changed her place,
  "Mother," she breathed, a smile grew on her face:
"Mother," my darling breathed, and slept content.

XX

There's one I miss. A little questioning maid
  That held my finger, trotting by my side,
  And smiled out of her pleased eyes open wide,
Wondering and wiser at each word I said.

———

And I must help her frolics if she played,
  And I must feel her trouble if she cried;
  My lap was hers past right to be denied;
She did my bidding, but I more obeyed.

Dearer she is to-day, dearer and more;
  Closer to me, since sister womanhoods meet;
Yet, like poor mothers some long while bereft,
I dwell on toward ways, quaint memories left,
  I miss the approaching sound of pit-pat feet,
The eager baby voice outside my door.

XXV

You think that you love each as much as one,
  Mothers with many nestlings 'neath your wings.
  Nay, but you know not. Love's most priceless things
Have unity that cannot be undone.
You give the rays, I the englobed full sun;
  I give the river, you the separate springs:
  My motherhood's all my child's with all it brings—
None takes the strong entireness from her: none.

You know not. You love yours with various stress;
  This with a graver trust, this with more pride;
This maybe with more needed tenderness:

————

I by each uttermost passion of my soul
Am turned to mine; she is one, she has the whole:
  How should you know who appraise love and divide?

XXVI

Of my one pearl so much more joy I gain
  As he that to his sole desire is sworn,
  Indifferent what women more were born,
And if she loved him not all love were vain,
Gains more, because of her—yea, through all pain,
  All love and sorrows, were they two forlorn—
  Than whoso happiest in the lands of morn
Mingles his heart amid a wifely train.

Oh! Child and mother, darling! Mother and child!
  And who but we? We, darling, paired alone?
  Thou hast all thy mother; thou art all my own.
  That passion of maternity which sweeps
Tideless 'neath where the heaven of thee hath smiled
  Has but one channel, therefore infinite deeps.

XXVII

Since first my little one lay on my breast
  I never needed such a second good,
  Nor felt a void left in my motherhood
She filled not always to the utterest.
The summer linnet, by glad yearnings pressed,
  Builds room enough to house a callow brood:
  I prayed not for another child—nor could;
My solitary bird had my heart's nest.

But she is cause that any baby thing
  If it but smile, is one of mine in truth,
  And every child becomes my natural joy:
And, if my heart gives all youth fostering,
  Her sister, brother, seems the girl or boy:
  My darling makes me mother to their youth.

AUGUSTA WEBSTER
[1837–1894]

THE OLD CRIB

"Sell that crib? Indeed! Indeed I cannot, for I see in it the faces of my children. I will starve before I sell that crib."

Confederate Lady, 1864.

I know thou art a senseless thing,
Still recollections round thee cling
Of joys long past;
And I would fain retain thee now,
Yet want's stern hand and lowering brow
Has o'er me cast
His misery with weight untold,
And, much prized crib, thou must be sold!

Ah! well do I remember yet,
Remember? can I well forget
That happy day,
When a swift tide my spirit moved,
And with a mother's soul, I loved
The child that lay
Within thy lap—my precious boy!
How throbbed my heart with untold joy.

How swiftly, then, the years sweep on,
With love, joy, wealth, they come, are gone,
And very soon
A little dark-eyed, bonny girl,
Pressed on thy pillow many a curl.

Most precious boon
That ever was to mortal given—
A cherub, from the gates of heaven.

And yet again, some powerful spell,
Called to this earth, sweet baby Bell,
My sunbeam child,
With hair of gold, and eyes of blue,
And cheeks that vie the rosebud's hue—
Pure, undefiled!

About my heart she seems to twine,
As round the oak, the clinging vine.

Take back thy gold! It shall not go!
'Twas mine in weal, and now in woe:
It comforts me.
It takes me back, in fitful gleams,
To the sweet, fairy land of dreams,
And then I see
Those little heads, with glossy curls,
My manly boy, my little girls!

MARY E. TUCKER
[1838–?]

MOTHERHOOD

From out the font of being, undefiled,
A life hath been upheaved with struggle and pain;
Safe in her arms a mother holds again
That dearest miracle—a new-born child.
To moans of anguish terrible and wild—
As shrieks the night-wind through an ill-shut pane—
Pure heaven succeeds; and after fiery strain
Victorious woman smiles serenely mild.

Yea, shall she not rejoice, shall not her frame
Thrill with a mystic rapture! At this birth,
The soul now kindled by her vital flame
May it not prove a gift of priceless worth?
Some saviour of his kind whose starry fame
Shall bring a brightness to the darkened earth.

MATHILDE BLIND
[1841–1896]

A MOTHER'S CALL

Come back, sons, over the sea!
Strong limbs I bore,
Ye are mine still!
Do you rise, do you move to me?
Do you hear there, across the tossing brine,
Sons?—for the great seas swell;
I smell the breath of them, I hear the roar of them,
Leaping, tossing, toppling over one another,
Lapping up to the shore,
Lashing the rock—furies,
What do they come for?
Sires of yours, yearsfull agonies—
Home with a wild lament?
Seas, is it this you bear?
No. But the times that come,
And the thunders I hear,
And the rent wide apart in her garment
That covered us, blinded us, wound us—
Chains ground that bound us,
That gyved us, sword that drank at our heart!

Leap to the rock, waves!
Leap to the land, sons, O braves!
Over graves, upon blood-trodden graves
Plant your feet!
Come, times, God-revenge,
Slow, sure, complete!

ELIZA KEARY
[19th century]

BABY EYES

*B*lue baby eyes, they are so sweetest sweet,
And yet they have not learned love's dear replies;
They beg not smiles, nor call for me, nor greet,
But clear, unshrinking, note me with surprise.
But, eyes that have your father's curve of lid,
You'll learn the look that he keeps somewhere hid:
You'll smile, grave baby eyes, and I shall see
The look your father keeps for only me.

AUGUSTA WEBSTER
[1837–1894]

A CHILD'S SMILE

"For I say unto you, that in heaven their angels do always
behold the face of my Father which is in heaven."

A child's smile—nothing more;
Quiet, and soft, and grave, and seldom seen;
Like summer lightning o'er,
Leaving the little face again serene.

I think, boy well-beloved,
Thine angel, who did grieve to see how far
Thy childhood is removed
From sports that dear to other children are,

On this pale cheek has thrown
The brightness of his countenance, and made
A beauty like his own—
That, while we see it, we are half afraid,

And marvel, will it stay?
Or, long ere manhood, will that angel fair,
Departing some sad day,
Steal the child-smile and leave the shadow care?

Nay, fear not. As is given
Unto this child the father watching o'er,
His angel up in heaven
Beholds Our Father's face for evermore.

And he will help him bear
His burthen, as his father helps him now:
So may he come to wear
That happy child-smile on an old man's brow.

DINAH MULOCK CRAIK
[1826–1887]

FROM AN OLD DOLL

*L*ow on her little stool she sits
To make a nursing lap,
And cares for nothing but the form
Her little arms enwrap.

With hairless skull that gapes apart,
A broken plaster ball,
One chipped glass eye that squints askew,
And ne'er a nose at all—

No raddle left on grimy cheek,
No mouth that one can see—
It scarce discloses, at a glance,
What it was meant to be.
. . . .
She rocks the scarecrow to and fro,
With croonings soft and deep,
A lullaby designed to hush
The bunch of rags to sleep.

I ask what rubbish has she there.
"My dolly," she replies,
But tone and smile and gesture say,
"My angel from the skies."

Ineffable the look of love
Cast on the hideous blur
That somehow means a precious face,
Most beautiful, to her.

The deftness and the tenderness
Of her caressing hands . . .
How can she possibly divine
For what the creature stands?

Herself a nurseling, that has seen
The summers and the snows
Of scarce five years of baby life.
And yet she knows—she knows.
. . . .
The majesty of motherhood
Sits on her baby brow;
Before her little three-legged throne
My grizzled head must bow.

That dingy bundle in her arms
Symbols immortal things—
A heritage, by right divine,
Beyond the claims of kings.

ADA CAMBRIDGE
[1844–1926]

HIS MOTHER

In the first dawn she lifted from her bed
The holy silver of her noble head,
And listened, listened, listened for his tread.
"Too soon, too soon!" she murmured, "Yet I'll keep
My vigil longer—thou, O tender Sleep,
Art but the joy of those who wake and weep!
Joy's self hath keen, wide eyes. O flesh of mine,
And mine own blood and bone, the very wine
Of my aged heart, I see thy dear eyes shine!
I hear thy tread; thy light, loved footsteps run
Along the way, eager for that 'Well done!'
We'll weep and kiss to thee, my soldier son!
Blest mother I—he lives! Yet had he died
Blest were I still,—I sent him on the tide
Of my full heart to save his nation's pride!
O God, if that I tremble so to-day,
Bowed with such blessings that I cannot pray
By speech—a mother prays, dear Lord, alway
In some far fibre of her trembling mind!
I'll up—I thought I heard a bugle bind
Its silver with the silver of the wind."

ISABELLA VALANCY CRAWFORD
[1850–1887]

HIS WIFE AND BABY

On the lone place of the leaves,
Where they touch the hanging eaves,
There sprang a spray of joyous song that sounded
      sweet and sturdy;
And the baby in the bed
Raised the shining of his head,
And pulled the mother's lids apart to wake and watch
      the birdie.
She kissed lip-dimples sweet,
The red soles of his feet,
The waving palms that patted hers as wind-blown
      blossoms wander;
He twined her tresses silk
Round his neck as white as milk—
"Now, baby, say what birdie sings upon his green spray
      yonder."
"He sings a plenty things—
Just watch him wash his wings!
He says Papa will march to-day with drums home
      through the city.
Here, birdie, here's my cup.
You drink the milk all up;
I'll kiss you, birdie, now you're washed like baby clean
      and pretty."
She rose, she sought the skies
With the twin joys of her eyes;
She sent the strong dove of her soul up through the
      dawning's glory;

She kissed upon her hand
The glowing golden band
That bound the fine scroll of her life and clasped her
      simple story.

ISABELLA VALANCY CRAWFORD
[1850–1887]

MOTHER AND CHILD

I saw a mother holding
Her play-worn baby son,
Her pliant arms enfolding
The drooping little one.
Her lips were made of sweetness,
And sweet the eyes above;
With infantile completeness
He yielded to her love.

And I who saw the heaving
Of breast to dimpling cheek,
Have felt, within, the weaving
Of thoughts I cannot speak;
Have felt myself the nestling,
All strengthless, love-enisled;
Have felt myself the mother
Abrood above her child.

ETHELWYN WETHERALD
[1857–1940]

31

FROM IN REFERENCE TO HER
CHILDREN, 23 JUNE 1659

I had eight birds hatcht in one nest,
Four Cocks were there, and Hens the rest.
I nurst them up with pain and care,
No cost nor labour did I spare
Till at the last they felt their wing,
Mounted the Trees and learned to sing.
. . . .
If birds could weep, then would my tears
Let others know what are my fears
Lest this my brood some harm should catch
And be surpris'd for want of watch
Whilst pecking corn and void of care
They fall un'wares in Fowler's snare;
Or whilst on trees they sit and sing
Some untoward boy at them do fling,
Or whilst allur'd with bell and glass
The net be spread and caught, alas;
Or lest by Lime-twigs they be foil'd;
Or by some greedy hawks be spoil'd.
O would, my young, ye saw my breast
And knew what thoughts there sadly rest.
Great was my pain when I you bred,
Great was my care when I you fed.
Long did I keep you soft and warm
And with my wings kept off all harm.
. . . .
When each of you shall in your nest
Among your young ones take your rest,

In chirping languages oft them tell
You had a Dame that lov'd you well,
That did what could be done for young
And nurst you up till you were strong
And 'fore she once would let you fly
She shew'd you joy and misery,
Taught what was good, and what was ill,
What would save life, and what would kill.
Thus gone, amongst you I may live,
And dead, yet speak and counsel give.
Farewell, my birds, farewell, adieu,
I happy am, if well with you.

ANNE BRADSTREET
[1612–1672]

TO A YOUNGER CHILD

*W*here sucks the bee now?—Summer is flying;
Leaves on the grass-plot faded are lying;
Violets are gone from the grassy dell,
With the cowslip-cups, where the fairies dwell;
The rose from the garden hath passed away—
Yet happy, fair boy! is thy natal day.

For love bids it welcome, the love which hath smiled
Ever around thee, my gentle child!
Watching thy footsteps, and guarding thy bed,
And pouring out joy on thy sunny head.
Roses may vanish, but this will stay—
Happy and bright is thy natal day.

FELICIA DOROTHEA HEMANS
[1793–1835]

TO A CHILD

I love to look on that eye of blue,
For tears have not yet worn a channel through;
And the few bright summers since thy birth,
Have left thee a stranger still on earth.

A stranger—and all, to thine untaught eyes,
Is bright with the hues of paradise.
The rapture of being thrills thy frame,
And sorrow thou know'st not even by name.

Thy innocent thoughts, unswayed by art,
Gush from the depths of thy guileless heart;
Like a harp when the wandering breezes sigh,
Answering each touch with melody.

I would, sweet one, I might wish for thee,
That a stranger thus thou shouldst ever be;
That time might not lift the enchanted veil,
Nor breathe in thine ear his mournful tale.

But those who are bid to this feast of life,
Must drink the cup,—must abide the strife:—
Then it were better to wish for thee,
Strength for the conflict, and victory.

ANNE C. LYNCH
[1815–1891]

35

TO MY GODCHILD ALICE

Alice, Alice, little Alice,
My new-christened baby Alice,
Can there ever rhymes be found
To express my wishes for thee
In a silvery flowing, worthy
Of that silvery sound?
Bonnie Alice, Lady Alice,
Sure, this sweetest name must be
A true omen to thee, Alice,
Of a life's long melody.

Alice, Alice, little Alice,
Mayst thou prove a golden chalice,
Filled with holiness like wine:
With rich blessings running o'er
Yet replenished evermore
From a fount divine:
Alice, Alice, little Alice,
When this future comes to thee,
In thy young life's brimming chalice
Keep some drops of balm for me!

Alice, Alice, little Alice,
Mayst thou grow a goodly palace,
Fitly framed from roof to floors,
Pure unto the inmost centre,
While high thoughts like angels enter
At the open doors:

Alice, Alice, little Alice,
When this beauteous sight I see,
In thy woman-heart's wide palace
Keep one nook of love for me.

Alice, Alice, little Alice,—
Sure the verse halts out of malice
To the thoughts it feebly bears,
And thy name's soft echoes, ranging
From quaint rhyme to rhyme, are changing
Into silent prayers.
God be with thee, little Alice,
Of His bounteousness may He
Fill the chalice, build the palace,
Here, unto eternity!

DINAH MULOCK CRAIK
[1826–1887]

A CHILD'S FANCY

❊

"Hush, hush! Speak softly, Mother dear,
So that the daisies may not hear;
For when the stars begin to peep,
The pretty daisies go to sleep.

"See, Mother, round us on the lawn,
With soft white lashes closely drawn,
They've shut their eyes so golden-gay,
That looked up through the long, long day.

"But now they're tired of all the fun—
Of bees and birds, of wind and sun
Playing their game at hide-and-seek—
Then very softly let us speak."

A myriad stars above the child
Looked down from heaven and sweetly smiled;
But not a star in all the skies
Beamed on him with his Mother's eyes.

She stroked his curly chestnut head,
And whispering very softly, said,
"I'd quite forgotten they might hear;
Thank you for that reminder, dear."

MATHILDE BLIND
[1841–1896]

———

MOTHER'S RECALL

Come back to me, O ye, my children;
Come back to the home as of yore;
As my longing eye peers through the vista of years,
Comes the heart-throbbing more and more.
I sit by the casement and listen
To the fall of the soft, sobbing rain,
E'en the winds gently sigh as if loth to reply—
In vain, fond mother, in vain.

Are ye gone for aye? Shall I no more hear
The ring and the din of glee?
Have my nestlings flown and left me alone?
Shall their faces, I no more see?
I sit, and I wait while the days go by,
And the months merge slow into years;
Till the twilight deep and the mystic sleep,
And the hopes give place to fears.

When the Christmas chimes with its holy rhymes
Ring out o'er the frosty plain,
Then I sit, and sigh for the "Sweet bye and bye"—
But the answer comes, "Mother in vain."
Each one of us, children, have gone forth
To fight out life's battles alone;
And the future must prove if your labor of love,
Has, like bread on the waters, been thrown.

So the twilight comes—and the fire burns low—
And the day is ebbing fast—
Soon the merry chimes and the hallowed rhymes
Will be numbered with the Past.
But with hopeful eyes I'll scan the skies,
Perchance, ere next Christmas-tide,
Will my children come to their own dear home.
And their place at mother's side.

MARY WESTON FORDHAM
[1862–?]

A MOTHER'S GRIEF AND JOY

$\mathcal{I}$ could not lift my voice to sing,
Nor touch my harp, to sweep a string;
And this world's joy and music seemed
As things whereof I had but dreamed.
For Death's pale angel stood so near
My only child, I could but Fear
And watch; or, bow my soul in prayer,
That He who governs Death, would spare
My tender infant's life—would save
My heart from bursting o'er its grave.

Ere yet twelve moons had silvered earth,
Since this bright being had its birth—
Before the soft, endearing word
Of "MOTHER," from its lips was heard,
The smiles that lit its beaming face
To marks of pain had given place.
Its cheek was wan, its languid eye
Rose feebly, as, to ask me why
I dropped from mine the tear of grief,
And did not give my babe relief.

The sides seemed overspread with gloom
Deep as the shades that fill the tomb,
And earth's bright blossoms, past away,
While my sweet flow'ret fading lay.
And, when I prayed—"Thy will be done!"
Strong nature cried, "O, be it one,

———

That shall my sinking babe restore!
And, Father, I will ask no more
Than that this froward will of mine
May here be swallowed up in thine!"

I know not how this double prayer
Of little faith and great despair,
Could e'er have reached the mercy-seat
A gracious answer there to meet!
But this sure word rebuked my fears,
"To reap in joy, ye sow in tears."
Then He, who gave it, heard my cries,
And caused the star of hope to rise
Upon my soul with cheering ray,
A blessed herald of the day.

And, since my heavenly Father smiled
Arid kindly gave me back my child,
The roses that its cheek resume
Have clothed the earth, to me, with bloom!
Its laughing eye to mine, is bright
Enough to fill the world with light!
There's music on the balmy air;
There's joy and glory every where!
I'll wake my harp—my voice I'll raise
And give to God my hymn of praise.

HANNAH FLAGG GOULD
[1789–1865]

———

HER LIKENESS

A girl, who has so many wilful ways
She would have caused Job's patience to forsake him;
Yet is so rich in all that's girlhood's praise,
Did Job himself upon her goodness gaze,
A little better she would surely make him.

Yet is this girl I sing in naught uncommon,
And very far from angel yet, I trow.
Her faults, her sweetnesses, are purely human;
Yet she's more lovable as simple woman
Than any one diviner that I know.

Therefore I wish that she may safely keep
This womanhede, and change not, only grow;
From maid to matron, youth to age, may creep,
And in perennial blessedness, still reap
On every hand of that which she doth sow.

DINAH MULOCK CRAIK
[1826–1887]

TO ANNIE

Annie, my first-born, gentle child,
My tender, fragile flower;
Why twines thy image round my heart,
With such mysterious power?

Is it because thy infant wail
The icy barrier moved,
That bound my soul's affections fast?
I knew 'twas mine I loved.

A mother's love no tongue can tell—
How boundless is that sea!
'Twas never mine; her spirit fled,
As she gave birth to me.

Annie, I gave to thee, my child,
The love my heart could yield;
God grant its influence o'er thee cast
From all life's ills a shield.

MARY E. TUCKER
[1838–?]

TO MY CHILDREN
(I THROUGH IV)

I

Shall I make a song for you,
  Children dear,
Not too hard or long for you,
  Just as clear
As your lives which opened so,
  A while ago?

How shall I find any word
  Old or new,
That the wise earth has not heard
  Ages through,
Ever since her ways grew sweet
  With little feet?

How you bless my day and hour,
  She can say,
As the sweet and spotless flower
  Of her May
Lies in fullest bloom at rest,
  Upon her breast.

All the happy service done,
  Well she knows,
All the longing, and the one
  Prayer that goes
Trembling through the unknown years,
  For you my dears.

How I love you, she repeats,
  How rejoice,
All my singing she completes,
  For my voice,
Of the song in her great heart,
  Is but a part.

II

Sleep, my little dearest one,
  I will guard thy sleep,
Safely little nearest one,
  I will hold thee deep,
In the dark unfathomed sea
Where sweet dreams are made for thee.

Rest my little baby dear,
  I will watch thy rest,
Thou shalt feel the waters near
  Only on my breast;

In the strong and tender tide,
Still my love shall be thy guide.

III

My little dear, so fast asleep,
  Whose arms about me cling,
What kisses shall she have to keep,
  While she is slumbering?

Upon her golden baby-hair,
  The golden dreams I'll kiss
Which Life spread through my morning fair,
  And I have saved, for this.

Upon her baby eyes I'll press
  The kiss Love gave to me,
When his great joy and loveliness
  Made all things fair to see.

And on her lips with smiles astir,
  Ah me, what prayer of old
May now be kissed to comfort her,
  Should Love or Life grow cold.

———

IV

Each morning, as the day begins,
  Her hair is sunlight to my eyes,
Each morning, as a new day wins
  The changeful skies.

In silken mist the tresses wind
  And float about her, while my hands
With loving care each day unbind
  The yellow strands.

And then a dancing cloud of gold
  Plays all around my darling's face,
Each morning while the days still hold
  My hour of grace.

And lightly, from my finger-tips,
  The sadness I no more can stay,
Into the golden glory slips,
  And dies away.

DOLLIE RADFORD
[1858–1920]

I I

Endearments from Daughters

TO MY FIRST LOVE, MY MOTHER

Sonnets are full of love, and this my tome
Has many sonnets: so here now shall be
One sonnet more, a love sonnet, from me
To her whose heart is my heart's quiet home,
To my first Love, my Mother, on whose knee
I learnt love-lore that is not troublesome;
Whose service is my special dignity,
And she my lodestar while I go and come.
And so because you love me, and because
I love you, Mother, I have woven a wreath
Of rhymes wherewith to crown your honored name:
In you not fourscore years can dim the flame
Of love, whose blessed glow transcends the laws
Of time and change and mortal life and death.

CHRISTINA ROSSETTI
[1830–1894]

51

SONGS FOR MY MOTHER
(I THROUGH IV)

My Mother's Clothes

When I was small, my mother's clothes
All seemed so kind to me!
I hid my face amid the folds
As safe as safe could be.

The gown that she had on
To me seemed shining bright,
For woven in that simple stuff
Were comfort and delight.

Yes, everything she wore
Received my hopes and fears,
And even the garments of her soul
Contained my smiles and tears.

Then softly will I touch
This dress she used to wear.
The old-time comfort lingers yet,
My smiles and tears are there.

A tenderness abides
Though laid so long away,
And I must kiss their empty folds,
So comfortable are they.

———

II

Her Hands

My mother's hands are cool and fair,
They can do anything.
Delicate mercies bide them there
Like flowers in the spring.

When I was small and could not sleep,
She used to come to me,
And with my cheek upon her hand
How sure my rest would be.

For everything she ever touched
Of beautiful or fine,
Their memories living in her hands
Would warm that sleep of mine.

Her hands remember how they played
One time in meadow streams,—
And all the flickering song and shade
Of water took my dreams.

Swift through her haunted fingers pass
Memories of garden things;—
I dipped my face in flowers and grass
And sounds of hidden wings.

One time she touched the cloud that kissed
Brown pastures bleak and far;—
I leaned my cheek into a mist
And thought I was a star.

All this was very long ago
And I am grown; but yet
The hand that lured my slumber so
I never can forget.

For still when drowsiness comes on
It seems so soft and cool,
Shaped happily beneath my cheek,
Hollow and beautiful.

III

Her Words

My mother has the prettiest tricks
Of words and words and words.
Her talk comes out as smooth and sleek
As breasts of singing birds.

She shapes her speech all silver fine
Because she loves it so.
And her own eyes begin to shine
To hear her stories grow.

And if she goes to make a call
Or out to take a walk,
We leave our work when she returns
And run to hear her talk.

We had not dreamed these things were so
Of sorrow and of mirth.
Her speech is as a thousand eyes
Through which we see the earth.

God wove a web of loveliness,
Of clouds and stars and birds,
But made not anything at all
So beautiful as words.

They shine around our simple earth
With golden shadowings,
And every common thing they touch
Is exquisite with wings.

There's nothing poor and nothing small
But is made fair with them.
They are the hands of living faith
That touch the garment's hem.

They are as fair as bloom or air,
They shine like any star,
And I am rich who learned from her
How beautiful they are.

IV

Her Stories

I always liked to go to bed—
It looked so dear and white.
Besides, my mother used to tell
A story every night.

When other children cried to go
I did not mind at all,
She made such faery pageants grow
Upon the bedroom wall.

The room was full of slumber lights,
Of seas and ships and wings,
Of Holy Grails and swords and knights
And beautiful, kind kings.

———

And so she wove and wove and wove
Her singing thoughts through mine.
I heard them murmuring through my sleep,
Sweet, audible, and fine.

Beneath my pillow all night long
I heard her stories sing,
So spun through the enchanted sheet
Was their soft shadowing.

Dear custom, stronger than the years—
Then let me not grow dull!
Still every night my bed appears
Friendly and beautiful!

Even now, when I lie down to sleep,
It comes like a caress,
And still somehow my childish heart
Expects a pleasantness.

I find in the remembering sheets
Old stories, told by her,
And they are sweet as rosemary
And dim as lavender.

ANNA HEMPSTEAD BRANCH
[1875–1935]

HIGH OR LOW

❁

For mother in lowly cabin, or mother in palace hall,
Is ever the truest and dearest, and ever the best of all.
Mother with hands toil-hardened, mother in pearls and
      lace,
The light of heavenly beauty shines in her tender face.

MARGARET ELIZABETH SANGSTER
[1838–1912]

———

BEAUTIFUL HANDS

Such beautiful, beautiful hands,
  They're neither white nor small;
And you, I know, would scarcely think
  That they were fair at all.
I've looked on hands whose form and hue
  A sculptor's dream might be,
Yet are these agéd wrinkled hands
  Most beautiful to me.

Such beautiful, beautiful hands!
  Though heart were weary and sad
These patient hands kept toiling on
  That the children might be glad.
I almost weep when looking back
  To childhood's distant day!
I think how these hands rested not
  When mine were at their play.

Such beautiful, beautiful hands!
  They're growing feeble now,
And time and pain have left their mark
  On hand, and heart and brow.
Alas! alas! the nearing time—
  And the sad, sad day to me,
When 'neath the daisies, out of sight,
  These hands must folded be.

But, oh! beyond the shadowy lands,
  Where all is bright and fair,
I know full well these dear old hands
  Will palms of victory bear;
When crystal streams, through endless years,
  Flow over golden sands,
And where the old are young again,
  I'll clasp my mother's hands.

EMMA M. H. GATES
[1835–1920]

MY MOTHER'S VOICE

*O*h never on my youthful ear
A Mother's gentle accents broke!
The vital spark, from which I sprung,
Expired, as I to life awoke.

No mother pressed me to her breast,
And bade my childish heart rejoice.
For with my infant first-born wail,
Death hushed for aye my mother's voice.

Alone I climbed the dizzy height,
That led to never-dying fame,
I sought and won, and now I wear
A famous, but unenvied name.

Had she been near, to shield and guide
Her wayward, but her trustful child,
Rare flowerets would have bloomed where now
Are weeds in rank luxuriance, wild.

In visions, sometimes, I behold
Her form of heavenly loveliness;
She speaks, and o'er me gently bends,
And prints on my pale brow a kiss.

And I awake—'tis but a dream!
But still the voice strikes on mine ear,
And from my callous heart calls forth
Up through mine eyes the scorching tear.

Then pass not judgment rash, or harsh,
On stern Misfortune's chosen child,
Who never heard a mother's voice,
On whom a mother never smiled!

MARY E. TUCKER
[1838–?]

A HAREBELL

Mother, if I were a flower
Instead of a little child,
I would choose my home by a waterfall,
To laugh at its gambols wild,—
To be sprinkled with spray and dew;—
And I'd be a harebell blue.

Blue is the color of heaven,
And blue is the color for me.
But in the rough earth my clinging roots
Closely nestled should be;
For the earth is friendly and true
To the little harebell blue.

I could not look up to the sun
As the bolder blossoms look;
But he would look up with a smile to me
From his mirror in the brook,
And his smile would thrill me through,—
A trembling harebell blue.

The winds would not break my stem
When they rushed in tempest by;
I would bend before them, for they come
From the loving Hand on high,
That never a harm can do
To a slender harebell blue.

I would play with shadow and breeze;
I would blossom from June till frost,
Dear mother, I know you would find me out,
When my stream-side cliff you crossed,
And I'd give myself to you,—
Your own little harebell blue.

LUCY LARCOM
[1824–1893]

MY MOTHER'S KISS

My mother's kiss, my mother's kiss,
I feel its impress now;
As in the bright and happy days
She pressed it on my brow.

You say it is a fancied thing
Within my memory fraught;
To me it has a sacred place—
The treasure house of thought.

Again, I feel her fingers glide
Amid my clustering hair;
I see the love-light in her eyes,
When all my life was fair.

Again, I hear her gentle voice
In warning or in love.
How precious was the faith that taught
My soul of things above.

The music of her voice is stilled,
Her lips are paled in death.
As precious pearls I'll clasp her words
Until my latest breath.

The world has scattered round my path
Honor and wealth and fame;
But naught so precious as the thoughts
That gather round her name.

And friends have placed upon my brow
The laurels of renown;
But she first taught me how to wear
My manhood as a crown.

My hair is silvered o'er with age,
I'm longing to depart;
To clasp again my mother's hand,
And be a child at heart.

To roam with her the glory-land
Where saints and angels greet;
To cast our crowns with songs of love
At our Redeemer's feet.

FRANCES E. W. HARPER
[1825–1911]

THE CHILD'S WISH IN JUNE

Mother, mother, the winds are at play,
Prithee, let me be idle to-day.
Look, dear mother, the flowers all lie
Languidly under the bright blue sky.
See, how slowly the streamlet glides;
Look, how the violet roguishly hides;
Even the butterfly rests on the rose,
And scarcely sips the sweets as he goes.
Poor Tray is asleep in the noon-day sun,
And the flies go about him one by one;
And pussy sits near with a sleepy grace,
Without ever thinking of washing her face.
There flies a bird to a neighbouring tree,
But very lazily flieth he,
And he sits and twitters a gentle note,
That scarcely ruffles his little throat.

You bid me be busy; but, mother, hear
How the hum-drum grasshopper soundeth near,
And the soft west wind is so light in its play,
It scarcely moves a leaf on the spray.
I wish, oh, I wish I was yonder cloud,
That sails about with its misty shroud;
Books and work I no more should see,
And I'd come and float, dear mother, o'er thee.

CAROLINE GILMAN
[1794–1888]

REMEMBRANCE OF CHILDHOOD

❊

The fire is blazing on the ample hearth,
Diffusing comfort through the antique room,
And we are watching in our simple mirth
The giant shadows starting from the gloom.

With seeming menace and imperious air
They seem to beckon with their wavering hands,
And flit away. We wonder whence they are,
And seek to reason of the ghostly bands.

But at our mother's voice we leave our play,
And crowd our low seats close around her chair;
Each prompt to meet the loving smiles that play
Upon her lips and brow so purely fair.

Her beautiful white hand forsakes awhile
The task by love made pleasant for our sake,
To rest a moment, with caressing wile,
On brows that 'neath that pressure could not ache.

Her clear eyes rest with proud yet troubled joy
Upon the blue-eyed treasures at her feet;
The rosy girl, the noble-hearted boy,
The little smilers, with their prattle sweet.

———

All good and happy, through her pious care,
Loving and well-beloved, a blessed band,
All leaning on her love, rejoiced to share
The blessings of her voice, her love, her hand.

And, now, our father, who, the whole day long,
Had plied the art by which he earns us bread,
With glance of pleasure on his own glad throng,
Sits down to taste the feast for reason spread.

His much-loved book—the poet's lofty lay,
The traveller's tale of strange and far-off lands,
The voyager's story of the mighty sea,
The attention of the little group commands.

We listen, full of wonder and delight,
Until the witching volume is laid by,
And loving voices breathe the kind "Good night!"
And light lids close above each sleepy eye.

LYDIA JANE PEIRSON
[1802–1862]

———

A MOTHER'S PICTURE

A lady, the loveliest ever the sun
Looked down upon you must paint for me:
Oh, if I only could make you see
The clear blue eyes, the tender smile,
The sovereign sweetness, the gentle grace,
The woman's soul, and the angel's face
That are beaming on me all the while,
I need not speak these foolish words:
Yet one word tells you all I would say,—
She is my mother: you will agree
That all the rest may be thrown away.

ALICE CARY
[1820–1871]

MY MOTHER

Give me my old seat, mother,
With my head upon thy knee;
I've pass'd through many a changing scene
Since thus I sat by thee.
Oh! let me look into thine eyes—
Their meek, soft, loving light
Falls, like a gleam of holiness,
Upon my heart to-night.

I've not been long away, mother;
Few suns have rose and set,
Since last the tear-drop on thy cheek
My lips in kisses met:
'T is but a little thee, I know,
But very long it seems,
Though every night I came to thee,
Dear mother, in my dreams.

The world has kindly dealt, mother,
By the child thou lov'st so well;
Thy prayers have circled round her path,
And 't was their holy spell
Which made that path so dearly bright,
Which strew'd the roses there,
Which gave the light, and cast the balm,
On every breath of air.

I bear a happy heart, mother,
A happier never beat;
And even now new buds of hope
Are bursting at my feet.
Oh, mother! life may be "a dream,"
But, if such *dreams* are given,
While at the portal thus we stand,
What are the *truths* of Heaven!

I bear a happy heart, mother,
Yet, when fond eyes I see,
And hear soft tones, and winning words,
I ever think of thee.
And then, the tear my spirit weeps
Unbidden fills my eye;
And, like a homeless dove, I long
Unto thy breast to fly.

Then, I am very sad, mother,
I'm very sad and lone;
Oh! there's no heart, whose inmost fold
Opes to me like thine own!
Though sunny smiles wreathe blooming lips,
While love-tones meet my ear;
My mother, one fond glance of thine
Were thousand times more dear.

———

Then, with a closer clasp, mother,
Now hold me to thy heart;
I'd feel it beating 'gainst my own
Once more before we part.
And, mother, to this love-lit spot,
When I am far away,
Come oft—*too oft* thou canst not come—
And for thy darling pray.

EMILY E. JUDSON
[1817–1854]

MY MOTHER'S PICTURE

How shall I here her placid picture paint
With touch that shall be delicate, yet sure?
Soft hair above a brow so high and pure
Years have not soiled it with an earthly taint,
Needing no aureole to prove her saint;
Firm mind that no temptation could allure;
Soul strong to do, heart stronger to endure;
And calm, sweet lips, that utter no complaint.

So have I seen her, in my darkest days
And when her own most sacred ties were riven,
Walk tranquilly in self-denying ways,
Asking for strength, and sure it would be given;
Filling her life with lowly prayer, high praise,—
So shall I see her, if we meet in heaven.

LOUISE CHANDLER MOULTON
[1835–1908]

THE OLD ARM-CHAIR

I love it, I love it; and who shall dare
To chide me for loving that old Arm-chair?
I've treasured it long as a sainted prize;
I've bedewed it with tears, and embalmed it with sighs.
'Tis bound by a thousand bands to my heart;
Not a tie will break, not a link will start.
Would ye learn the spell?—a mother sat there;
And a sacred thing is that old Arm-chair.

In Childhood's hour I lingered near
The hallowed seat with listening ear;
And gentle words that mother would give;
To fit me to die, and teach me to live.
She told me shame would never betide,
With truth for my creed and God for my guide;
She taught me to lisp my earliest prayer;
As I knelt beside that old Arm-chair.

I sat and watched her many a day,
When her eye grew dim, and her locks were grey:
And I almost worshipped her when she smiled,
And turned from her Bible, to bless her child.
Years rolled on; but the last one sped—
My idol was shattered; my earth-star fled:
I learnt how much the heart can bear,
When I saw her die in that old Arm-chair.

'Tis past, 'tis past, but I gaze on it now
With quivering breath and throbbing brow:
'Twas there she nursed me; 'twas there she died:
And Memory flows with lava tide.
Say it is folly, and deem me weak,
While the scalding drops start down my cheek;
But I love it, I love it; and cannot tear
My soul from a mother's old Arm-chair.

ELIZA COOK
[1818–1889]

TO MY MOTHER

(Written in her sixteenth year.)

O thou whose care sustained my infant years,
And taught my prattling lip each note of love;
Whose soothing voice breathed comfort to my fears,
And round my brow hope's brightest garland wove;

To thee my lay is due, the simple song,
Which Nature gave me at life's opening day;
To thee these rude, these untaught strains belong,
Whose heart indulgent will not spurn my lay.

O say, amid this wilderness of life,
What bosom would have throbbed like thine for me?
Who would have smiled responsive?—who in grief,
Would e'er have felt, and feeling, grieved like thee?

Who would have guarded, with a falcon eye,
Each trembling footstep or each sport of fear?
Who would have marked my bosom bounding high,
And clasped me to her heart, with love's bright tear?

Who would have hung around my sleepless couch,
And fanned, with anxious hand, my burning brow?
Who would have fondly pressed my fevered lip,
In all the agony of love and woe?

———

None but a mother—none but one like thee,
Whose bloom has faded in the midnight watch;
Whose eye, for me, has lost its witchery,
Whose form has felt disease's mildew touch.

Yes, thou hast lighted me to health and life,
By the bright lustre of thy youthful bloom—
Yes, thou hast wept so oft o'er every grief,
That woe hath traced thy brow with marks of gloom.

O then, to thee, this rude and simple song,
Which breathes of thankfulness and love for thee,
To thee, my mother, shall this lay belong,
Whose life is spent in toil and care for me.

LUCRETIA MARIA DAVIDSON
[1808–1825]

GRANNY

Here, in her elbow chair, she sits
A soul alert, alive,
A poor old body shrunk and bent—
The queen-bee of the hive.

But hives of bees and hives of men
Obey their several laws;
No fiercely-loving filial throng
This mother-head adores.

This bringer of world-wealth, whereof
None may compute the worth,
Is possibly of no account
To anyone on earth.

Her cap and spectacles, that mean
Dim eyes and scanty hairs,
The humble symbols of her state—
The only crown she wears.

Lacking a kingdom and a court,
A relic of the past,
Almost a cumberer of the ground—
That is our queen at last.

But still not wholly without place,
Nor quite bereft of power;
A useful stopgap—a resource
In many a troubled hour.

She darns the stockings, keeps the house,
The nurseless infant tends,
While the young matrons and the men
Pursue their various ends—

Too keen-set on their great affairs,
Or little plays and pranks,
The things and people of their world,
To give her thought or thanks—

The children on whom all her thought
And time and love were spent
Through half a century of years!
Yet is she well content.

The schooling of those fiery years,
It has not been for nought;
A large philosophy of life
Has self-less service taught.

The outlook from the heights attained
By climbings sore and slow
Discovers worlds of wisdom, hid
From clearest eyes below.

———

So calmly, in her elbow chair,
Forgotten and alone,
She knits and dreams, and sometimes sighs
But never makes a moan.

Still dwelling with her brood unseen—
Ghosts of a bygone day—
The precious daughter in her grave,
The dear son gone astray—

And others, to whom once she stood
As only light and law,
The near and living, and yet lost,
That need her love no more.

Watching their joyous setting forth
To mingle with their kind,
With scarce a pang, with ne'er a grudge,
At being left behind.

"Let them be young, as I was young,
And happy while they may" . . . .
A dog that waits the night in peace
Since it has had its day.

ADA CAMBRIDGE
[1844–1926]

ON MY MOTHER'S BIRTH-DAY

Clad in all their brightest green,
This day the verdant fields are seen;
The tuneful birds begin their lay,
To celebrate thy natal day.
The breeze is still, the sea is calm,
And the whole scene combines to charm;
The flowers revive, this charming May,
Because it is thy natal day.
The sky is blue, the day serene,
And only pleasure now is seen;
The rose, the pink, the tulip gay,
Combine to bless thy natal day.

FELICIA DOROTHEA HEMANS
[1793–1835]

TO MY MOTHER

Mother! thou bid'st me touch the lyre,
  And wake its sweetest tones for thee;
To kindle fancy's dying fire,
  And light the torch of poetry.

Mother! how sweet the word, how pure,
  As if from heaven the accents came;
If aught can rouse the dormant soul,
  It is that cherish'd, honour'd name.

Deep in the heart's recess it dwells;
  It lives with being's earliest dawn;
With reason's light expands and swells,
  And dies with parting life alone.

Mother! 't is childhood's first essay,
  Breathed in its trembling tones of love;
It lights the heart, through life's long way,
  And points to holier worlds above!

It is a name, whose mighty spell
  Can draw the chain'd affections forth,
Can rouse the feelings from their cell,
  And give each purer impulse birth.

Then will I wake my sleeping muse,
  And strive to breathe my thoughts in song,
Though sweetest strains must fail to speak
  The heart's affections, deep and strong.

MARGARET MILLER DAVIDSON
[1787–1844]

FROM DEDICATION. TO MY MOTHER

The flowers of romance that I cherished,
  Around me lie withered and dead;
The stars of my youth's shining heaven,
  Were but meteors whose brightness misled;
And the day-dreams of life's vernal morning,
  Like the mists of the morning have fled.

But one flower I have found still unwithered;
  Like the night-scented jasmin it gleams;
And beyond where the fallen stars vanished,
  One light pure and hallowed still beams;
One love I have found, deep and changeless,
  As that I have yearned for in dreams.

Too often the links have been broken,
  That bound me in friendship's bright chain
Too often has fancy deceived me
  To blind or to charm me again;
And I sigh o'er my young heart's illusions,
  With a sorrow I would were disdain.

But now, as the clouds return earthward,
  From the cold and void ether above;
As on pinions all drooping and weary,
  O'er the waste flew the wandering dove;
O'er the tide of the world's troubled waters,
  I return to the ark of thy love.

———

Here, at length, my tired spirit reposes;
  Here my heart's strongest tendrils entwine;
Here its warmest and deepest affections
  It lays on earth's holiest shrine;
Dearest mother, receive the devotion
  Of the life thou hast given from thine.

ANNE C. LYNCH
[1815–1891]

ROCK ME TO SLEEP

Backward, turn backward, O Time, in your flight,
Make me a child again just for tonight!
Mother, come back from the echoless shore,
Take me again to your heart as of yore;
Kiss from my forehead the furrows of care,
Smooth the few silver threads out of my hair;
Over my slumbers your loving watch keep;—
Rock me to sleep, mother,—rock me to sleep!

Backward, flow backward, O tide of the years!
I am so weary of toil and of tears—
Toil without recompense, tears all in vain—
Take them, and give me my childhood again!
I have grown weary of dust and decay—
Weary of flinging my soul-wealth away;
Weary of sowing for others to reap;—
Rock me to sleep, mother,—rock me to sleep!

Tired of the hollow, the base, the untrue,
Mother, O mother, my heart calls to you!
Many a summer the grass has grown green,
Blossomed and faded, our faces between;
Yet with strong yearning and passionate pain,
Long I to-night for your presence again.
Come from the silence so long and so deep;—
Rock me to sleep, mother,—rock me to sleep!

Over my heart, in the days that are flown,
No love like mother-love ever has shone;
No other worship abides and endures—
Faithful, unselfish, and patient like yours:
None like a mother can charm away pain
From the sick soul and the world-weary brain.
Slumber's soft calms o'er my heavy lips creep;—
Rock me to sleep, mother,—rock me to sleep!

Come, let your brown hair, just lighted with gold,
Fall on your shoulders again as of old;
Let it drop over my forehead to-night,
Shading my faint eyes away from the light;
For with its sunny-edged shadows once more
Haply will throng the sweet visions of yore;
Lovingly, softly, its bright billows sweep:—
Rock me to sleep, mother,—rock me to sleep!

Mother, dear mother, the years have been long
Since I last listened your lullaby songs:
Sing, then, and unto my soul it shall seem
Womanhood's years have been only a dream.
Clasped to your heart in a loving embrace,
With your light lashes just sweeping my face,
Never hereafter to wake or to weep;—
Rock me to sleep, mother,—rock me to sleep!

ELIZABETH AKERS ALLEN
[1832–1911]

THE SHEPHERDESS

She walks—the lady of my delight—
  A shepherdess of sheep.
Her flocks are thoughts. She keeps them white;
  She keeps them from the steep;
She feeds them on the fragrant height,
  And folds them in for sleep.

She roams maternal hills and bright,
  Dark valleys safe and deep.
Into that tender breast at night
  The chastest stars may peep.
She walks—the lady of my delight—
  A shepherdess of sheep.

She holds her little thoughts in sight,
  Though gay they run and leap.
She is so circumspect and right;
  She has her soul to keep.
She walks—the lady of my delight—
  A shepherdess of sheep.

ALICE CHRISTIANA MEYNELL
[1847–1922]

FRONTISPIECE OF AN ALBUM
FILLED WITH THE WORKS OF ART
OF THREE SISTERS FOR THEIR MOTHER

As on a lake the water-flow'rs arise,
  Nurs'd by its bosom to the forms they wear,
And floating o'er it, paint it with their dyes,
  And shed a tribute of their perfume there;
So, mother, by thy cares all gently brought
  From the dark nothingness of infancy,
  And in our folded youth, inspired by thee
To shine in talent, or expand in thought,
We offer to thee, like the thankful flow'rs,
  An image of the minds that by thee live;
And in the incense of their open'd pow'rs,
Return a tribute back of that which thou didst give.

"V" (CAROLINE WIGLEY CLIVE)
[1801–1873]

*N*ature, the gentlest mother,
Impatient of no child,
The feeblest or the waywardest,—
Her admonition mild

In forest and the hill
By traveller is heard,
Restraining rampant squirrel
Or too impetuous bird.

How fair her conversation,
A summer afternoon,—
Her household, her assembly;
And when the sun goes down

Her voice among the aisles
Incites the timid prayer
Of the minutest cricket,
The most unworthy flower.

When all the children sleep
She turns as long away
As will suffice to light her lamps;
Then, bending from the sky

With infinite affection
And infiniter care,
Her golden finger on her lip,
Wills silence everywhere.

EMILY DICKINSON
[1830–1886]

MY MOTHER

*W*ho fed me from her gentle breast
And hushed me in her arms to rest,
And on my cheek sweet kisses prest?
    My mother.

When sleep forsook my open eye,
Who was it sung sweet lullaby
And rocked me that I should not cry?
    My mother.

Who sat and watched my infant head
When sleeping in my cradle bed,
And tears of sweet affection shed?
    My mother.

When pain and sickness made me cry,
Who gazed upon my heavy eye
And wept, for fear that I should die?
    My mother.

Who ran to help me when I fell
And would some pretty story tell,
Or kiss the part to make it well?
    My mother.

Who taught my infant lips to pray,
To love God's holy word and day,
And walk in wisdom's pleasant way?
    My mother.

And can I ever cease to be
Affectionate and kind to thee
Who wast so very kind to me,—
    My mother.

Oh no, the thought I cannot bear;
And if God please my life to spare
I hope I shall reward thy care,
    My mother.

When thou art feeble, old and gray,
My healthy arm shall be thy stay,
And I will soothe thy pains away,
    My mother.

And when I see thee hang thy head,
'Twill be my turn to watch thy bed,
And tears of sweet affection shed,—
    My mother.

JANE TAYLOR
[1783–1824]

———

SONNET, TO MY MOTHER

To thee, maternal guardian of my youth,
  I pour the genuine numbers free from art;
The lays inspir'd by gratitude and truth,
  For thou wilt prize th' effusion of the heart.
Oh! be it mine, with sweet and pious care,
  To calm thy bosom in the hour of grief;
With soothing tenderness to chase the tear,
  With fond endearments to impart relief.
Be mine thy warm affection to repay
  With duteous love in thy declining hours;
  My filial hand shall strew unfading flowers,
Perennial roses to adorn thy way:
Still may thy grateful children round thee smile,
Their pleasing care affliction shall beguile.

FELICIA DOROTHEA HEMANS
[1793–1835]

MY BLESSED MOTHER

My Blessed Mother dozing in her chair
On Christmas Day seemed an embodied Love,
A comfortable Love with soft brown hair
Softened and silvered to a tint of dove;
A better sort of Venus with an air
Angelical from thoughts that dwell above;
A wiser Pallas in whose body fair
Enshrined a blessed soul looks out thereof.
Winter brought holly then; now Spring has brought
Paler and frailer snowdrops shivering;
And I have brought a simple humble thought—
I her devoted duteous Valentine—
A lifelong thought which drills this song I sing.
A lifelong love to this dear saint of mine.

CHRISTINA ROSSETTI
[1830–1894]

I I I

Endearments from Sons

YOU PAINTED NO MADONNAS

*Y*ou painted no Madonnas
On chapel walls in Rome;
But with a touch diviner
You lived one in your home.
You wrote no lofty poems
That critics counted art;
But with a nobler vision,
You lived them in your heart.

You carved no shapeless marble
To some high soul design
But with a finer sculpture
You shaped this soul of mine.
You built no great cathedrals
That centuries applaud;
But with a grace exquisite
Your life cathedraled God.
Had I the gift of Raphael
Or Michelangelo
O what a rare Madonna
My mother's life would show.

THOMAS FESSENDEN
[1771–1837]

WHAT IS HOME WITHOUT A MOTHER?

*W*hat is home without a mother?
What are all the joys we meet?
When her loving smile no longer
Greets the coming of our feet?
The days are long, the nights are drear,
And time rolls slowly on;
And oh, how few are childhood's pleasures,
When her loving care is gone.

SEPTIMUS WINNER
[1827–1902]

THE HAND THAT ROCKS THE CRADLE IS THE HAND THAT RULES THE WORLD

*B*lessings on the hand of women!
Angels guard its strength and grace,
In the palace, cottage, hovel,
Oh, no matter where the place;
Would that never storms assailed it,
Rainbows ever gently curled;
For the hand that rocks the cradle
Is the hand that rules the world.

Infancy's the tender fountain,
Power may with beauty flow,
Mother's first to guide the streamlets,
From them souls unresting grow—
Grow on for the good or evil,
Sunshine streamed or evil hurled;
For the hand that rocks the cradle
Is the hand that rules the world.

Woman, how divine your mission
Here upon our natal sod!
Keep, oh, keep the young heart open
Always to the breath of God!
All true trophies of the ages
Are from mother-love impearled;
For the hand that rocks the cradle
Is the hand that rules the world.

Blessings on the hand of women!
Fathers, sons, and daughters cry,
And the sacred song is mingled
With the worship in the sky—
Mingles where no tempest darkens,
Rainbows evermore are hurled;
For the hand that rocks the cradle
Is the hand that rules the world.

WILLIAM ROSS WALLACE
[1819–1881]

THE GREATEST BATTLE
THAT EVER WAS FOUGHT

The greatest battle that ever was fought—
  Shall I tell you where and when?
On the maps of the world you will find it not:
  It was fought by the Mothers of Men.

Not with cannon or battle shot,
  With sword or nobler pen;
Not with eloquent word or thought
  From the wonderful minds of men;

But deep in a walled up woman's heart;
  A woman that would not yield;
But bravely and patiently bore her part;
  Lo! there is that battlefield.

No marshalling troops, no bivouac song,
  No banner to gleam and wave;
But Oh these battles they last so long—
  From babyhood to the grave!

But faithful still as a bridge of stars
  She fights in her walled up town;
Fights on, and on, in the endless wars;
  Then silent, unseen goes down!

Ho! ye with banners and battle shot,
　　With soldiers to shout and praise,
I tell you the kingliest victories fought
　　Are fought in these silent ways.

JOAQUIN MILLER
[1841-1913]

LULLABY, GO TO SLEEP

I'll ne'er forget the day,
When I was young and gay,
A rolling 'round the floor in Tennessee;
From th' cotton field so white,
My ma would come at night,
And fondly hold me in her arms and say:

Go to sleep, baby mine,
Little birdie in your nest;
Humming bees have left the vine,
Go to sleep and take your rest.

In winter cold and chill,
At night, when all was still,
I'd wake to find her standing over me,
A smile upon her face,
A creepin 'round the place,
She'd tuck the cover over me, and sing:

Go to sleep, baby mine,
Little birdie in your nest;
Humming bees have left the vine,
Go to sleep and take your rest.

So many years have passed,
Since we assembled last,
That dear old soul has gone away to dwell.
If this whole world was mine,

———————

The wealth I would decline,
If I could only hear my mother sing:

Go to sleep, baby mine,
Little birdie in your nest;
Humming bees have left the vine,
Go to sleep and take your rest.

JAMES E. McGIRT
[1874–1930]

———

TO MY MOTHER

*B*ecause I feel that, in the Heavens above,
  The angels, whispering to one another,
Can find, among their burning terms of love,
  None so devotional as that of "Mother,"
Therefore by that dear name I long have called you—
  You who are more than mother unto me,
And fill my heart of hearts, where Death installed you
  In setting my Virginia's spirit free.
My mother—my own mother, who died early,
  Was but the mother of myself; but you
Are mother to the one I loved so dearly,
  And thus are dearer than the mother I knew
By that infinity with which my wife
  Was dearer to my soul than its soul-life.

EDGAR ALLAN POE
[1809–1849]

MY TRUST

A picture memory brings to me:
I look across the years and see
Myself beside my mother's knee.
I feel her gentle hand restrain
My selfish moods, and know again
A child's blind sense of wrong and pain.
But wiser now, a man gray grown,
My childhood's needs are better known,
My mother's chastening love I own.

JOHN GREENLEAF WHITTIER
[1807–1892]

BETTER MOMENTS

My mother's voice! how often creep
Its accents o'er my lonely hours!
Like healing sent on wings of sleep,
Or dew to the unconscious flowers.
I can forget her melting prayer
While leaping pulses madly fly;
But in the still, unbroken air
Her gentle tones come stealing by,
And years, and sin, and manhood flee,
And leave me at my mother's knee.

The book of nature, and the print
Of beauty on the whispering sea,
Give aye to me some lineament
Of what I have been taught to be.
My heart is harder, and perhaps
My manliness hath drunk up tears,
And there's a mildew in the lapse
Of a few miserable years—
But nature's book is even yet
With all my mother's lessons writ.

I have been out at eventide
Beneath a moonlit sky of spring,
When earth was garnish'd like a bride,
And night had on her silver wing—
When bursting leaves and diamond grass,
And waters leaping to the light,

———

And all that make the pulses pass
With wilder fleetness, throng'd the night;
When all was beauty—then have I,
With friends on whom my love is flung,
Like myrrh on winds of Araby,
Gazed up where evening's lamp is hung.
And when the beauteous spirit there
Flung over me its golden chain,
My mother's voice came on the air,
Like the light dropping of the rain,
Shower'd on me from some silver star:
Then, as on childhood's bended knee,
I've poured her low and fervent prayer,
That our eternity might be
To rise in heaven like stars at night,
And tread a living path of light.

I have been on the dewy hills,
When night was stealing from the dawn,
And mist was on the waking rills,
And tints were delicately drawn
In the gray east—when birds were waking
With a slow murmur in the trees,
And melody by fits was breaking
Upon the whisper of the breeze,
And this when I was forth, perchance,
As a worn reveller from the dance—
And when the sun sprang gloriously

———

And freely up, and hill and river
Were catching upon wave and tree
The subtile arrows from his quiver—
I say a voice has thrilled me then,
Heard on the still and rushing light,
Or, creeping from the silent glen
Like words from the departing night,
Hath stricken me, and I have press'd
On the wet grass my fever'd brow,
And pouring forth the earliest,
First prayer, with which I learn'd to bow,
Have felt my mother's spirit rush
Upon me as in by-past years,
And yielding to the blessed gush
Of my ungovernable tears,
Have risen up—the gay, the wild—
As humble as a very child.

NATHANIEL PARKER WILLIS
[1806–1867]

———

A MOTHER'S PICTURE

She seemed an angel to our infant eyes!
Once, when the glorifying moon revealed
Her who at evening by our pillow kneeled—
Soft-voiced and golden-haired, from holy skies
Flown to her loves on wings of Paradise—
We looked to see the pinions half-concealed.
The Tuscan vines and olives will not yield.
Her back to me, who loved her in this wise,
And since have little known her, but have grown
To see another mother, tenderly,
Watch over sleeping darlings of her own;
Perchance the years have changed her; yet alone
This picture lingers: still she seems to me
The fair, young Angel of my infancy.

EDMUND CLARENCE STEDMAN
[1833–1908]

THE MOTHER'S HYMN

"Blessed art thou among women."

*L*ord who ordainest for mankind
Benignant toils and tender cares,
We thank thee for the ties that bind
The mother to the child she bears.

We thank thee for the hopes that rise
Within her heart, as, day by day,
The dawning soul, from those young eyes,
Looks with a clearer, steadier ray.

And grateful for the blessing given
With that dear infant on her knee,
She trains the eye to look to heaven,
The voice to lisp a prayer to Thee.

Such thanks the blessed Mary gave
When from her lap the Holy Child,
Sent from on high to seek and save
The lost of earth, looked up and smiled.

All-Gracious! grant to those who bear
A mother's charge, the strength and light
To guide the feet that own their care
In ways of Love and Truth and Right.

WILLIAM CULLEN BRYANT
[1794–1878]

FROM REVERIE

*B*ut God is sweet.
My mother told me so,
When I knelt at her feet
Long—so long—ago;
She clasped my hands in hers.
Ah! me, that memory stirs
My soul's profoundest deep—
No wonder that I weep.
She clasped my hands and smiled,
Ah! then I was a child—
I knew not harm—
My mother's arm
Was flung around me; and I felt
That when I knelt
To listen to my mother's prayer,
God was with mother there.

Yea! "God is sweet!"
She told me so;
She never told me wrong;
And through my years of woe
Her whispers soft, and sad, and low,
And sweet as Angel's song,
Have floated like a dream.
. . . .

FR. ABRAM J. RYAN
[1838–1886]

Fond mourner! be that solace thine!
　Let hope her healing charm impart,
And soothe, with melodies divine,
　The anguish of a mother's heart.
O, think! the darlings of thy love,
　Divested of this earthly clod,
Amid unnumber'd saints above,
　Bask in the bosom of their God.

Of their short pilgrimage on earth
　Still tender images remain:
Still, still they bless thee for their birth,
　Still filial gratitude retain.
Each anxious care, each rending sigh,
　That wrung for them the parent's breast,
Dwells on remembrance in the sky,
　Amid the raptures of the blest.

O'er thee, with looks of love, they bend;
　For thee the Lord of life implore;
And oft, from sainted bliss descend,
　Thy wounded quiet to restore.
Oft, in the stillness of the night,
　They smooth the pillow of thy bed;
Oft, till the morn's returning light,
　Still watchful hover o'er thy head.

Hark! in such strains as saints employ,
  They whisper to thy bosom peace;
Calm the perturbed heart to joy,
  And bid the streaming sorrow cease.
Then dry, henceforth, the bitter tear:
  Their part and thine inverted see:—
Thou wert their guardian angel here,
  They guardian angels now to thee.

JOHN QUINCY ADAMS
[1767–1848]

MOTHER AND CHILD

Charles, my slow heart was only sad, when first
I scanned that face of feeble infancy;
For dimly on my thoughtful spirit burst
All I had been, and all my babe might be!
But when I saw it on its Mother's arm,
And hanging at her bosom (she the while
Bent o'er its features with a tearful smile),
then I was thrilled and melted, and most warm
Impressed a Father's kiss; and all beguiled
Of dark remembrance, and presageful fear,
I seemed to see an Angel's form appear—
'Twas even thine, beloved Woman mild!
So for the Mother's sake the Child was dear,
And dearer was the Mother for the Child.

SAMUEL TAYLOR COLERIDGE
[1772–1839]

TO THE NEW WOMEN

Free to look at fact,
Free to come and go,
Free to think and act,
Now you surely know
The wrongs of womanhood
At last are fairly dead.

Abler than man to vex,
Less able to be good,
Fiercer in your sex,
Wilder in your mood,
Seeking—who knows what?
About the world you grope;
Some of you have thought
Man may be your hope.

Soon again you'll see,
Love and love alone,
As simple as can be,
Can make this life atone.

Be bold and yet be bold,
But be not overbold,
Although the knell is tolled
Of the tyranny of old.

And meet your splendid doom,
On heaven-scaling wings,
Women, from whose bright womb
The radiant future springs!

JOHN DAVIDSON
[1857–1909]

TO ALISON CUNNINGHAM
FROM HER BOY

For the long nights you lay awake
And watched for my unworthy sake;
For your most comfortable hand
That led me through the uneven land;
For all the story-books you read;
For all the pains you comforted;
For all you pitied, all you bore,
In sad and happy days of yore;
My second Mother, my first Wife,
The angel of my infant life—
From the sick child, now well and old,
Take, nurse, the little book you hold!

And grant it, Heaven, that all who read
May find as dear a nurse at need,
And every child who lists my rime,
In the bright, fireside, nursery clime,
May hear it in as kind a voice
As made my childish days rejoice!

ROBERT LOUIS STEVENSON
[1850–1894]

———

TO MY MOTHER

Chiming a dream by the way
  With ocean's rapture and roar,
I met a maiden today
  Walking alone on the shore;
Walking in maiden wise,
  Modest and kind and fair,
The freshness of spring in her eyes
  And the fullness of spring in her hair.

Cloud-shadow and scudding sun-burst
  Were swift on the floor of the sea,
And a mad wind was romping its worst,
  But what was their magic to me?
Or the charm of the midsummer skies?
  I only saw she was there,
A dream of the sea in her eyes
  And the kiss of the sea in her hair.

I watched her vanish in space;
  She came where I walked no more;
But something had passed of her grace
  To the spell of the wave and the shore;
And now, as the glad stars rise,
  She comes to me, rosy and rare,
The delight of the wind in her eyes
  And the hand of the wind in her hair.

WILLIAM ERNEST HENLEY
[1849–1903]

A MOTHER UNDERSTANDS

*W*hen mother sits beside my bed
At night, and strokes and smooths my head,
And kisses me, I think, some way,
How naughty I have been all day;
Of how I waded in the brook,
And of the cookies that I took,
And how I smashed a window light
A-rassling—me and Bobby White—
And tore my pants, and told a lie;
It almost makes me want to cry
When mother pats and kisses me;
I'm just as sorry as can be,
But I don't tell her so—no, sir.
She knows it all; you can't fool her.

ANONYMOUS

INDEX OF AUTHORS

INDEX
OF FIRST LINES

ABOUT THE AUTHOR

With a degree in English literature, KATHLEEN BLEASE first served as an editor for two major publishing houses before starting out on her own as a freelance book editor and writer. Over the span of her career, she has written on a variety of topics—from health to education to home improvements to parenthood—and edited books that have won acclaim throughout the country.

Five years ago, her love unexpectedly knocked on her front door and introduced himself, and Kathleen's vision of life changed forever. Today she is a full-time mother of two small boys, often writing and researching with a little one in her arms. Marriage, motherhood, and faith—and their powerful lessons—are often the focus of her essays, articles, and collections.

Kathleen's first collection, *Love in Verse: Classic Poems of the Heart,* is a Boston Book Review bestseller. Her other collection is *A Friend Is Forever: Precious Poems That Celebrate the Beauty of Friendship.*

She lives with her husband, Roger, and their two children in the historic district of Easton, Pennsylvania.